Davy Crockett

A Photo-Illustrated Biography

by Kathy Feeney

Consultant:
Ken Tester
Ranger
Davy Crockett Birthplace State Park
Limestone, Tennessee

Bridgestone Books
an imprint of Capstone Press
Mankato, Minnesota

Bridgestone Books are published by Capstone Press
151 Good Counsel Drive, P.O. Box 669, Mankato, Minnesota 56002
http://www.capstone-press.com

Library of Congress Cataloging-in-Publication Data
Feeney, Kathy, 1954–
    Davy Crockett: a photo-illustrated biography/by Kathy Feeney.
    p. cm.—(Photo-illustrated biographies)
    Includes bibliographical references and index.
    Summary: A brief biography of the frontiersman and statesman from Tennessee who died
at the Alamo.
    ISBN 0-7368-1110-9
    1. Crockett, Davy, 1786–1836—Juvenile literature. 2. Crockett, Davy, 1786–1836—Pictorial
works—Juvenile literature. 3. Pioneers—Tennessee—Biography—Juvenile literature.
4. Tennessee—Biography—Juvenile literature. 5. Legislators—United States—Biography
Juvenile literature. 6. United States. Congress. House—Biography—Juvenile literature.
7. Alamo (San Antonio, Tex.)—Siege, 1836—Juvenile literature. [1. Crockett, Davy, 1786–1836.
2. Pioneers. 3. Legislators.] I Title. II. Series.
F436.C95 F44 2002
976.8′04′092—dc21   2001005422

Editorial Credits
Gillia Olson, editor; Karen Risch, product planning editor; Timothy Halldin, cover
    designer; Steve Christensen, interior layout designer; Alta Schaffer, photo researcher

Photo Credits
Bettmann/CORBIS, 4
Burstein Collection/CORBIS, 16
Crockett Tavern Museum/Sally B. Bennett, 8
Hulton/Archive Photos, 10, 14, 18, 20
North Wind Picture Archives, 12
Pat O'Hara/CORBIS, 6
Stock Montage, Inc., cover

**The author wishes to dedicate this book to the readers at Seminole Elementary School in
Tampa, Florida.**

1 2 3 4 5 6 07 06 05 04 03 02

Table of Contents

King of the Wild Frontier

Some people call Davy Crockett "King of the Wild Frontier." Davy enjoyed exploring new places. He often told tall tales about his adventures. These stories stretched the truth.

Davy had no formal education. But he still accomplished much during his lifetime. Davy served with Andrew Jackson during the War of 1812 (1812–1815). Davy was elected to the U.S. Congress as a Tennessee representative. He also fought at the Alamo to try to free Texas from Mexico.

Davy was famous for his coonskin caps. Historians disagree on how often he wore these furry hats. But drawings showed him wearing a coonskin cap during his time in Congress. Davy enjoyed public service. But he preferred his adventures in the wilderness.

Davy was known for his wilderness adventures.

Childhood

Davy was born on August 17, 1786, in a log cabin near Limestone, Tennessee. His parents were John and Rebecca Crockett. They grew corn and raised hogs. They worked hard.

Davy loved to wander in the woods. He had his own bow and arrow when he was 5 years old. He hunted animals for family meals. He also caught fish and collected honey. Davy dreamed of growing up to be a great hunter.

The Crocketts struggled to make money. They often moved, trying to find a better life. The Crocketts once built a mill. A mill is a factory that grinds crops into meal. But a flood washed the mill away.

Davy's parents opened the Crockett Tavern when he was 10 years old. People rented rooms and bought food and drinks at this inn. Davy met many travelers there who taught him how to tell stories.

Davy was born in a log cabin. This cabin was rebuilt and now is part of a Tennessee state park.

1B **9**
CROCKETT TAVERN

Here stood the Crockett Tavern, established and operated by John and Rebecca Crockett. It was the boyhood home of David Crockett (1786-1836), pioneer and political leader in Tennessee, and a victim of the Alamo Massacre at San Antonio, Texas.

Growing Up

When Davy was 12 years old, a traveler came to the tavern. He needed help herding cattle to Virginia. Davy's father told the man that Davy could do the job. The man hired Davy. Davy had never been away from his family. He saw that there was a big country to explore.

Davy's parents sent him to school when he returned. Davy was not used to a classroom. He did not like to be indoors all day. Davy got into fights at school. He left school after four days. But Davy knew his father would be angry. Davy decided to run away from home rather than face his father's anger.

On his own, Davy's life was tough. He picked crops, pushed a plow, worked on a wagon train, and made hats. Davy lived in the woods and had to hunt deer and other wildlife for food. He stayed away from home for three years.

The Crockett Tavern was rebuilt and now contains a museum.

A New Family

Davy returned home when he was 16. In the early 1800s, most young men worked for their father. Davy worked for people to whom his father owed money. He also received a few months of basic education from one of his employers.

At age 18, Davy met Mary "Polly" Finley at a dance. He and Polly married on August 14, 1806. They moved to Mulberry Creek near Lynchburg, Tennessee. Davy built a log house. He hunted deer, bears, and wolves. Davy sold the animals' skins for money. Polly and Davy had two sons and a daughter. They were John, William, and Margaret.

In 1813, Davy joined the Tennessee militia to fight with General Andrew Jackson in the War of 1812. Davy fought most of his battles against American Indians. He came to respect the American Indians. He realized they were fighting to keep their homeland.

Davy was a scout in the Tennessee militia during the War of 1812.

Life Changes

Davy returned home to Polly after the war. But Polly died in 1815. Davy later married Elizabeth Patton. She was a widow who had a son and a daughter. Davy and Elizabeth had three more children. They were Robert, Rebecca, and Matilda.

Davy and Elizabeth owned and operated a gristmill. This water-powered machine ground corn into cornmeal. People use cornmeal to make cornbread.

Davy became known in his town as a hunter, a soldier, and a storyteller. People liked to listen to Davy's tall tales. He told these stories in exciting ways. He often made up parts of the stories.

Davy also became involved in public service. He became a justice of the peace in 1817. In this job, he performed marriages and decided court cases.

Davy and Elizabeth's gristmill may have looked like this one, located in Tennessee.

"I can outspeak any man on this floor and give him two hours start. I can outlook a panther, outstare a flash o' lightnin', tote a steamboat on my back, and play at rough and tumble with a lion..."
–Davy, in one of his speeches to Congress

Crockett in Congress

Davy ran for the state legislature of Tennessee in 1821. At the time, he did not know much about politics. But people liked his funny and exciting speeches. He won the election. He was reelected to the legislature in 1823.

Davy ran for U.S. Congress in 1827. From 1827 to 1831, Davy served as a U.S. representative from Tennessee. He served another term from 1833 to 1835. Some people called Davy the "Coonskin Congressman." He got this name because of his rough manners and country background. People drew him wearing coonskin caps.

In Congress, Davy fought for people's rights to own their homes. People in Tennessee had settled free government land. Davy did not want a few wealthy men wanted to take over the property. Davy also spoke up for American Indians in the southeast. He did not want settlers to force them off their land.

Davy's funny speeches helped him win a seat in the Tennessee state legislature.

"I must say as to what I have seen of Texas it is the garden spot of the world. The best land and the best prospects for health I ever saw, and I do believe it is a fortune to any man to come here. There is a world of country to settle here,"
–Davy, in a letter, January 9, 1836

Texas Bound

Davy became tired of politics. Many people did not agree with him on settlement and American Indian issues. But many of the same people still liked him.

Davy's life of adventure made him famous around the country. People also enjoyed his stories. In 1834, he wrote *The Narrative of the Life of David Crockett of the State of Tennessee*. Thomas Chilton helped him write this book. It was about Davy's adventures in the Tennessee frontier.

Davy missed his adventures. He decided to move to Texas. Texas was a new frontier. Not many people lived there. Davy decided it would be a good place for him to live. His family planned to follow once Davy was settled.

Texas was not a state when Davy moved there in 1835. Mexico ruled parts of Texas. This situation caused tension between the U.S. settlers and the Mexican government.

People often drew Davy wearing a coonskin cap in Congress. But Davy usually dressed in a suit.

Remember the Alamo

English-speaking Texans wanted to break free from Mexico and form a separate country. The Mexican government sent troops to Texas to try to stop these rebels. Davy joined the rebels as a volunteer soldier. An old mission served as a military fort. This building was run by religious people. It is called the Alamo.

On February 22, 1836, about 3,000 Mexican soldiers surrounded the Alamo. Davy was one of about 180 men defending the fort. The Texans protected the fort for 12 days. They hoped help was on its way. But the help that came was not enough. Davy and all the Texans at the Alamo were killed.

People all over Texas honored these rebels with the famous quote "Remember the Alamo!" This battle cry inspired others to continue the fight to free Texas. They succeeded. Texas became independent from Mexico a few weeks later.

Davy is shown on the right holding a rifle over his head while fighting at the Alamo.

A Legendary Life

Davy Crockett was a legendary person. Many people remember tall tales about him. One of these legends says that Davy killed a bear when he was 3 years old. Another says he fought a cougar. Many of the things people say about Davy may not have been true. But these legends are exciting.

After his death, people published the "Davy Crockett Almanacs." These books contained information about crops and the weather. They also included tall tales about Davy and other heroes.

Davy's legend has been told in books and movies. During the 1950s, many children watched a TV show about Davy Crockett.

Several historic sites mark important places in Davy's life. His childhood home is now a state park. The Crockett Tavern has been restored. The Crockett Museum holds items from Davy's life.

Stories about Davy told about him as a tough man.

Fast Facts about Davy Crockett

 According to one tall tale, Davy killed 49 bears in just one month with his rifle "Old Betsy."

 Davy preferred to be called by his legal name, David. He signed legal documents David Crockett.

 Davy's tombstone reads, "Davy Crockett, Pioneer, Patriot, Soldier, Trapper, Explorer, State Legislator, Congressman, Martyred at The Alamo. 1786–1836."

Dates in Davy Crockett's Life

1786—Davy is born August 17 in Green Country, Tennessee.

1799—Davy runs away from home.

1806—Davy marries Mary "Polly" Finley.

1813—Davy serves with the Tennessee militia during the War of 1812.

1815—Polly dies; Davy marries Elizabeth Patton.

1817—Davy becomes a justice of the peace.

1821—Davy is elected to the Tennessee State Legislature.

1827—Davy becomes a U.S. Congressman.

1835—Davy moves to Texas.

1836—Davy dies on March 6 defending the Alamo.

Words to Know

Alamo (AL-uh-moh)—a San Antonio, Texas, fort that had once been a mission; it was the site of a battle to free Texas from Mexican rule.

almanac (AWL-muh-nak)—a yearly magazine or book that contains facts and information

Congress (KONG-griss)—a government body that creates and passes laws; Congress is made up of the Senate and the House of Representatives

coonskin (KOON-skin)—the skin and fur of a raccoon that can be made into a hat

frontier (fruhn-TIHR)—the far edge of a country where few people live

legend (LEJ-uhnd)—a story handed down from earlier times; legends often are based on fact, but they are not completely true.

legislature (LEJ-iss-lay-chur)—a group of people who make laws for a country or state

militia (muh-LISH-uh)—a group of citizens who are trained to fight, but who only serve in an emergency

wilderness (WIL-dur-niss)—a wild area where few or no people live

Read More

Adler, David A. *A Picture Book of Davy Crockett.* New York: Holiday House, 1998.

Johnston, Marianne. *Davy Crockett.* American Legends. New York: PowerKids Press, 2001.

Useful Addresses

Crockett Museum
1300 West Gaines (Highway 64)
Lawrenceburg, TN 38464

Davy Crockett Birthplace
  State Park
1245 Davy Crockett Park Road
Limestone, TN 37681-5825

Internet Sites

American West on Davy Crockett
http://www.americanwest.com/pages/davycroc.htm
Davy Crockett Birthplace State Park
http://www.state.tn.us/environment/parks/davyshp
Handbook of Texas Online: David Crockett
http://www.tsha.utexas.edu/handbook/online/articles/view/CC/
    fcr24.html

Index